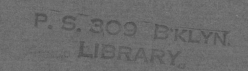

DESIGNING THE FUTURE

Published by Creative Education
123 South Broad Street, Mankato, Minnesota 56001
Creative Education is an imprint of The Creative Company

Designed by Stephanie Blumenthal

Photographs by Melinda Belter, Michelle Burgess, Corbis-Bettmann, Don Eastman,
John Elk III, Nihat Iyriboz, Kim Karpeles, Craig Lovell, Eugene G. Schulz,
Tom Till Photography, and Tom Stack and Associates

Library of Congress Cataloging-in-Publication Data

Halfmann, Janet.
Theaters / by Janet Halfmann
p. cm. — (Designing the future)
Includes index
Summary: Examines the history, building, structure, and uses of various theater buildings around
the world and describes some notable examples.
ISBN 0-88682-720-5
1. Theater architecture—History—Juvenile literature. [1. Theater architecture—History.
2. Theaters—History.] I. Title. II. Series.
NA6821.H16   1999
725'.822'09—dc21   98-35274

First Edition

2   4   6   8   9   7   5   3   1

DESIGNING THE FUTURE

THEATERS

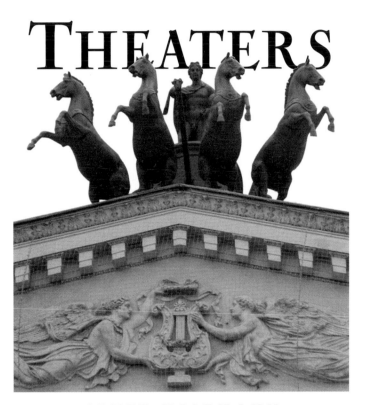

JANET HALFMANN

CREATIVE EDUCATION

Holiday sounds filled the London air in 1598 as the actor Richard Burbage, his brother, and the master carpenter Peter Street took down the Theater. The men and their helpers had a big job to do—secretly and quickly, but with care, so the timbers could be reused.

The brothers hoped to cart the timbers away before the landlord returned from holiday. The brothers' late father had built the Theater on rented land. The landlord, who wouldn't renew the lease, threatened to take over the building.

Interior of the First Theatre, Covent Garden

Rumors spread about Burbage's secret project to dismantle the Theater, and the landlord sent a man to investigate. Peter Street tricked the man, showing him how carefully the workers were marking every board. That proved, Street explained, that they planned to construct a different building on the very same spot. The man believed him. Then at midnight, about 30 men hauled the boards across the river, where the rebuilding could begin. This would be a

Aspendos theater at Antalya, Turkey

SHAKESPEARE

He was not of an age, but for all time.
—*fellow playwright Ben Jonson*

new theater named the Globe—the most famous play-

house ever built—for the most famous playwright who

ever lived, William Shakespeare.

The staging of plays started in many places of

the world as songs and dances to honor ancient gods.

The festivals in Athens, Greece, in the sixth century B.C.

attracted people from all over the Greek world. The

Greeks built their theaters on hillsides near temples.

Early theaters were constructed of wood, later ones of

stone. These were large enough to hold the entire city,

Aspendos Theater, Antalya, Turkey

and the plays presented lasted all day. The bleacher-like seating was called the *theatron*, which means "seeing place." The seating surrounded three sides of a round playing area at the bottom of the hill called the orchestra, or orchestra pit.

Behind the orchestra was a scene building called a *skene*, which gave us the modern word "scene." It was a dressing room for the actors and a backdrop for the action. The scene wall gradually became more elaborate. It had three entries, repre-

The honored plays of ancient Greek dramatists, such as Euripides, are still performed in the theater at Epidaurus. Sound carries so well here that if a match is struck at the bottom of the hill in the orchestra, its sound can be heard in the farthest seat away.

senting the city, country, and a palace or temple. A high, raised stage was added between the scene wall and the orchestra. The actors performed on the stage, and a group of dancers and singers called the chorus used the orchestra below. Painted panels of scenery were set up between pillars supporting the front of the stage.

When the Romans conquered Greece in the second century B.C., they adopted its theater. They lowered the stage and added more details to the scene wall. But unlike the Greeks, they

Ruins of Arykanda, Turkey

built the theater on flat ground. They reduced the seating to a semi-circle and joined it to the scene wall, so the entire theater was enclosed by walls. Inside the Roman theaters, the dramas were filled with action, violence, bloodshed, and rough humor. Church leaders disliked the horrors shown in the theaters and eventually closed them. For more than 1,000 years, no new theaters were built. Instead storytellers, jugglers, and minstrels traveled from town to town, performing

The Colosseum, Rome

on makeshift stages. By the mid-16th century, religious drama had lost popularity, and audiences were flocking to see skillful performances by professional acting companies in Spain, Italy, and England.

In England, the acting companies performed in the large yards of inns. People stood on balconies or in the yard to watch the plays. The players set up boards on barrels for a stage. Later, permanent theaters were

THE GLOBE

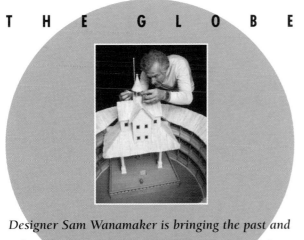

Designer Sam Wanamaker is bringing the past and future together, building an exact replica of the Globe Theater

London's Shaftsbury Avenue

modeled after the inn yards. The most famous of these permanent theaters, the Globe, could hold 3,000 people. William Shakespeare wrote most of his 37 plays for its stage. It was a black-and-white, or timber-frame, building—the most common at that time in England. Lime, sand, and cow's hair were mixed together to make plas-

Greek actors wore masks that told the audience the character's mood. Eventually, the wide upturned mouth on the mask for comedy and the wide downturned mouth on the mask for tragedy became worldwide symbols for the theater, seen on posters and signs.

ter to fill in the walls, and reeds were woven together to make a thatched roof a foot or more thick. The Globe had a polygon shape with 20 sides—almost circular. It was 100 feet (30.5 m) across and 36.5 feet (11 m) tall. Two staircase towers extended out on its sides. Inside the theater, workers placed the raised stage with its back to

Barbican Center in London, England

the afternoon sun. That way players wouldn't have to squint, since all plays were in the afternoon. The stage was five feet (1.5 m) high and jutted out about halfway into the open yard.

Two tall columns supported the roof over the stage; they were painted to resemble marble. The ceiling over the stage was painted sky-blue and decorated

Spain had a golden age of drama at about the same time as England. The most popular dramas were "cape and sword" plays. Sword-carrying actors swirled their capes for disguise or to express emotions.

with stars—it was called the heavens. Trap doors in the floor were used so that devils, ghosts, smoke, and mist could rise up from a hidden area under the stage. Players could also descend, as if into a dungeon or grave. At the back of the stage, a small, curtained room was perfect for showing sur-prises—a treasure, a tomb, a dead body. Players came

The Kennedy Center, Washington, D.C.

New Opera House, Paris, France

on stage through entrances on either side of this recess. Above the stage, workers built a gallery for battle or balcony scenes, such as in Shakespeare's *Romeo and Juliet*. Behind the stage, the permanent scene wall, with entrances and windows to the stage, was decorated like London buildings of the time. The backstage area was behind the scene wall.

Richard Wagner's Festspielhaus was the first to lower the lights and hide the musicians from the audience. He made these changes to enhance the illusion of reality on stage and to prevent distractions.

At the very top of the theater, workers built a space for creating sound effects, such as rolling a cannon ball on a metal sheet for thunder. Here, too, the trumpet player sounded the start of the play. A flagpole stood at the very top. On play days, a flag flew high for everyone in London to see. People of all classes flocked to the daily two

15

o'clock performances. Then, on June 29, 1613, disaster struck. A cannon was fired during a play, and a spark landed in the thatch on the roof. In less than an hour, the Globe burned to the ground. Amazingly, no one was hurt. The players decided right away to rebuild the Globe. By the next summer, a second Globe, more splendid than the first, had opened. This time, the roof was tiled. The new Globe delighted its audiences until 1642, when it was shut down by the religious laws of the Puritans and later torn down.

La Scala Opera House, Milan, Italy

In June 1997, 400 years after the first Globe stood in London, another new Globe opened near the original site. Architects and builders used oak timbers, plaster, and thatch just as Peter Street did in 1599—but they made the thatch fire-proof and installed a sprinkler system. The plays of Shakespeare and other playwrights of his time, as well as contemporary plays, are being performed on the same stage setting just as they were 400 years ago.

In Italy in the 1500s, Sebastiano Serlio was the first to design realistic movable sets. He painted scenes in perspective on panels, angling them along both sides of a back stage that tilted up. Grooves for the panels allowed scenes to be changed quickly.

Several other theaters imitate Shakespeare's Globe, such as the Globe of the Great Southwest in Odessa, Texas, and the Elizabethan stage of the Oregon Shakespeare Festival in Ashland, Oregon.

The Teatro Olimpico, built in Vicenza, Italy, in the 1580s, had the first permanent set designed to look

The Globe Theatre, London, England

Olympic Theater, Vicensa, Italy

Academy of Music, Philadelphia (above)
Mann's Chinese Theater, Los Angeles (below)

real. It was created by the famous Italian architect Andrea Palladio. When he died years later, Palladio's pupil, Vincenzo Scamozzi, took over the work of set designing. Today, the Teatro Olimpico still stands and is Europe's oldest existing indoor theater. In 1618, Architect G. B. Aleotti designed the Farnese Theater in Parma, Italy. His construction was unique, however. Called the proscenium, or picture-frame theater, its design is commonly used today. In this theater, an

SPECIAL EFFECTS

Even in ancient Greece, special effects delighted the audience. Ropes were used to lower actors to the stage, and the sound of thunder was recreated.

arch, or frame, forms a large opening in the center of the scene wall. The audience looks through this opening to watch the action. Aleotti's theater was also the first designed for movable scenery. This magnificent theater can still be seen in the Pilotta Palace in Parma, Italy.

A major change in theater architecture in the 19th century took place at the Festspielhaus (Festival Theater) in Bayreuth, Germany. This 1876 theater was designed by the great composer Richard Wagner, who wanted everyone in his audience to see and hear equally from any seat. To accomplish this, the theater building has no balconies or private boxes; rather, all seats are arranged in a single sloping block designed in a fan shape. This type of seating is used today in most movie theaters to accommodate all people.

The three most common designs for theater

Royal Opera House, London

21

Lincoln Center, New York City

stages are the proscenium, thrust, and arena. The proscenium, or picture-frame, stage is by far the most common. In this kind of theater, the stage is framed by an arch. The audience looks through the picture-frame opening onto the stage. Most of the theaters on Broadway in New York City have proscenium stages, as do many schools. The thrust stage is also known as an open or platform stage. This stage extends into the audience, which is seated on three sides, allowing many of the spectators to be close to the action. Good examples are the Tyrone Guthrie Theater in Minneapolis, Minnesota, which has a unique seven-sided thrust stage; and the Olivier Theater in the Royal National Theater complex in London, England. A

Architect William Tuthill wasn't in Carnegie Hall for its grand opening program. He had stopped in earlier, seen the crowd in the balconies, and worried whether the supports would hold. He rushed home to check his math, wanting to ensure that he had not made a mistake. He hadn't, and Carnegie Hall still stands firmly.

third stage design is the arena, also known as theater-in-the-round. It has seating all around a stage or floor area in the center. This is usually a smaller and more personal theater, with the audience close to the stage. Arena Stage in Washington, D.C., has an 800-seat theater-in-the-round; and the Stephen Joseph

Interior of the London Theater

Theater in Scarborough, England, has a 404-seat theater called The Round.

Theaters are created in many architectural styles all around the world. The 1900 New Victory Theater in New York City is the oldest existing Broadway theater. Lincoln Center covers four blocks in New York City and can seat 18,000 people at one time in its various halls. The center's five buildings of glass and stone surround a central plaza with a

Radio City Music Hall, New York City

Theater organ in Radio City Music Hall

fountain. The gigantic Metropolitan Opera House, with its six-story glass lobby looking out through five arched windows, dominates the plaza. Large brilliant-colored murals cover the lobby's two front walls, and a grand staircase spirals up to five red and gold balconies in the auditorium. Radio City Music Hall in New York City's Rockefeller Center is the world's largest indoor theater, with 6,200 seats. Its proscenium arch is repeated across the ceiling to look like the rising sun. The huge stage of the 1932 theater measures 144 by 69 feet (44 by 21 m). Floor-to-ceiling mirrors in the lobby reflect glistening chandeliers, and a grand staircase fills the end wall. The Apollo Theater is a cultural landmark in the heart of Harlem. Since 1934 it has been a popular stage for black entertainers such as Ella Fitzgerald, Duke Ellington, Aretha

Apollo Theater in Harlem, New York City

Franklin, Ray Charles, Little Richard, and Stevie Wonder. Carnegie Hall is one of the world's most celebrated music halls. The 3,000-seat hall opened in 1891 with a concert conducted by the Russian composer Tchaikovsky.

The Paris Opera in France was built to be a symbol of national glory.

The first Greek plays were called tragedies, from the Greek word *tragos,* the name given to the goat sacrificed at the festival honoring Dionysus. Greek tragedies often showed human conflict with the gods.

When it opened in 1875, it became the largest, most glamorous, and best-known opera house in the world, with a grand staircase, masses of sculptures and glittering chandeliers, and three domes. For more than 100 years, it was home to the Paris Opera, which now performs in the new Opera Bastille.

Opera House in Paris, France (opposite); Moscow's Bolshoi Theater, founded in 1919 (above)

Entrance to Ford's Theater, Washington, D.C.

Today the Paris Opera, also known as the Opera Garnier, still stages operas and dance. The famous Bolshoi Theater in Moscow, Russia, has an eight-column portico, or roofed entranceway, crowned by a large bronze statue of Apollo, the god of the arts, driving his chariot. The original theater, built in 1824, was damaged by fire and reconstructed in 1856. The Bolshoi Theater is home to the internationally acclaimed Bolshoi Ballet.

Ford's Theater in Washington, D.C., looks just like it did the evening in 1865 when President Abraham Lincoln was shot by John Wilkes Booth. The president's box is decorated with a red sofa, American flags, and a picture of George Washington. The popular theater was ordered closed after the assassination, and no one performed on its stage for more than 100 years. In 1968 it was completely restored and reopened.

Interior of Ford's Theater

Kabuki theater

In 1925, the Kabuki-za was built in Tokyo, Japan, specifically for performing *kabuki*, a traditional Japanese play that combines drama, dance, and music. The 2,600-seat Kabuki-za has a runway that passes through the audience from the back of the theater to the revolving stage. The actors make spectacular entrances and exits by this runway and also perform on it. In the kabuki theater, the proscenium stage is wider than in a regular theater and the auditorium is more shallow because it's important for the actor to be close to the audience. Kabuki was started in the early 17th century by women. Today it is performed only by men wearing colorful costumes, wigs, and heavy makeup. Mann's Chinese Theater in Hollywood, California, is the most famous movie palace in the world. The lavish 1927 theater looks like a Chinese fantasy, with huge red piers in front and an immense

A Kabuki theater in Kyoto, Japan

Sydney Opera House

sculpted stone dragon. Almost 200 performers have left their handprints, footprints, and signatures in the cement courtyard in front of the theater.

Sydney Opera House in Australia appears to be sailing into the harbor like a majestic ship. Its white "sails" billow 230 feet (60 m) into the sky. The 1973 opera house, with its futuristic design, is the internationally recognized symbol of Australia. The impressive building, which took 14 years to build, is considered one of the most beautiful buildings in the world.

Today, no flags fly and no trumpets blare to call us to the theater as in the time of Shakespeare's Globe. Thanks to architects and builders, though, historic theaters and new buildings alike are home to players around the world who are waiting to entertain an admiring audience.

Stairway up to the balcony

INDEX